# This Nest, Swift *Passerine*

# This Nest, Swift *Passerine*

*A* Poem | Dan Beachy-Quick

T|P

TUPELO PRESS
North Adams, Massachusetts

# Acknowledgments

Thank you to the editors of the following journals who were kind enough to publish this work: *Cutbank, Gulf Coast, Parakeet, The Sonora Review,* and *Watershed.*

Thank you to Srikanth Reddy and Suzanne Buffam, for guidance and patience. Thank you Mai Wagner for conversations and support. Thank you Donald Revell for vision and advice. Thank you Becky Beachy for the example of your own work.

*Nota Bene:* The italicized text in *This Nest, Swift Passerine* is taken from other sources, a list of which appears in the "Notes."

*This Nest, Swift Passerine*

ISBN 978-1-932195-60-6
LCCN: 2008907828

Cover painting, "Robin's Nest," by David Kroll.
Cover and text design by Howard Klein.

First paperback edition April 2009

Printed in the United States.

Tupelo Press
P.O. Box 1767
Eclipse Mill, 243 Union Street, Loft 305
North Adams, Massachusetts 01247
Telephone: (413) 664-9611 / Fax: (413) 664-9711
editor@tupelopress.org / www.tupelopress.org

Tupelo Press is an award-winning independent literary press that publishes fine fiction, non-fiction and poetry in books that are as much a joy to hold as they are to read. Tupelo Press is a registered 501(c)3 non-profit organization and relies on donations to carry out its mission of publishing extraordinary work that may be outside the realm of the large commercial publisher.

 Supported in part by an award from the National Endowment for the Arts

For Hana and Kristy—
*the Wounded Deer—leaps highest*

# Contents

Here we find ourselves, suddenly, not in critical
speculation, but in a holy place, and should
go warily and reverently. We stand before the
secret of the world, there where Being passes
into Appearance, and Unity into Variety.

—Emerson

First

1—

The daily all everywhere disclosed

—

But how find how    *as it flew onward*
*& the mountains gave back the sound*
to say what I mean    *the call of the bird*
*& the echoe after*   to say I've seen?

Raven hungers and calls and the mountain
Hungers back and calls
The whole range of peaks in the bird's beak.
Raven lonely and the mountain rings
Loneliness & *the echoe after we could see*
*him no longer*

The echo after we could see    Light in echo the eye sees
also through the ear           a double infinity

—

A particle of light in the sun's center—so densely Labyrinthine is the star—takes
1,000,000 years to reach the sun's surface.

8 minutes from the sun's surface to my eye.

The eye is made of the light by which it sees. Every eye, and all the world which
enters through the pin-hole of the eye, is 1,000,000 years and 8 minutes old.

—

My amber eye in this amber world
Sees wind seize the cloud and straighten
The cloud and with one gust circle
The cloud into itself as a dolphin
Diving into its own reflection is a circle
Before the cloud is gone

The sky ripples from the vision
Not of time but in time
The accident clear as now disclosed
How much of vision is memory

If not all the snow
Trace left on each needle of pine

When wind bursts
Through the tree the tree breathes
Out its own echo in the air

I see two trees hovering in the air

And the echo world nests in nothing
Save its own sudden existence
In wind that ceasing now lets drift
The snow pine down onto the frozen
Lake     *the lake was most still*

Witness the still lake in my eye
Lake where witness is ice and thaw

—

*floating on the water*
*it <u>seemed</u> in the wood*

your gale in me seemed
to double me and break me

in clear hemispheres

—one grave, one light—

the ever ripening ancient

—

This past winter 75 percent of the monarch population froze to death on the trees in which they nested. Those that survived had to climb through the collision of dead butterflies atop them and fly thousands of miles north.

In the city where I live the main avenues are divided by medians filled with marigolds. Marigolds are the same color as monarchs and the monarchs feed on them.

The city buses speed down the avenue as the monarchs sift down to the flowers. Each one dead from that collision would be one less of the dwindling whole. I feared for them; I could not turn away. Every time a monarch floated down in front of the speeding bus the air the bus pushed in front of it pushed the monarch to safety, a dozen feet above the danger, and it fluttered back down to pollen to sip. "Plashless."

Such a bright day that day the monarchs arrived. The escape from harm within the harm itself.

—

Leaning over the water I see my own

Reflection not the surface

Where my eye is open to my eye

But deeper in the water where light

Ripples on current and current

The lake pulls to depths

Gravity and Light move at the same speed. The fruit occurs in my eye as quickly as the force that through the fruit will force it to fall.

—

*Hang there like fruit, my soul,*
*Till the tree die!*

—

what

falls we see

is revealed we say what is

is quicker than light is

quicker than

gravity

—

*The lake was most still & reflected the beautiful yellow & blue & purple & grey colours of the sky. We heard a strange sound in the Bainriggs wood as we were floating on the water it <u>seemed</u> in the wood, but it must have been above it for presently we saw a raven very high above us—it called out & the Dome of the sky seemed to echoe the sound—it called again & again as it flew onwards, & the mountains gave back the sound, seeming as if from their center a musical bell-like answering to the birds hoarse voice. We heard both the call of the bird & the echoe after we could see him no longer.*

A fine wild innocence not ease
We hear when we cannot see
The wooddeep shade where the *aster* grows
*Wm went into the wood to compose*

—

*William cut wood a little     Wm wrote out part of his poem & endavoured
to alter it, & so made himself ill     William composing in the wood in the
morning     William had slept better. He fell to work, & made himself unwell
William sadly tired & working still     William was very unwell, worn out
with his bad nights rest—he went to bed, I read to him to endeavour to make
him sleep     William slept well but his tongue is feverish*

—

Dorothy writes of whom and what she loves for sake of whom she loves. Referring
to herself she sometimes confuses pronouns, writing *he* when she means to say *I*. She
witnesses Wm's cost at composing poems: illness, sleeplessness, irritable despair. She
writes of the leaves forced by wind off the tree. Dorothy records moment after moment
in which she hears that which she cannot see—the ear vicariously become the eye.

I've mistaken wind coursing through leaves in the forest for a river that does not exist.
*River* cognate to *Rive*. A river between what I thought true and what was true. A river
within my mind. *To rive* also means *to cleave together.* Each leaf a pond. Each tree a lake.
Wind ripples every surface and makes each still surface seem alive.

Form falsely orders when order is false. Spent months above the blank page unable to
find a word more interesting than the blank it would mar. Then winter. Then winter
arrived. Each tree pinned against sky. To be honest in writing to those I love—

—

*William was disturbed in the night by the rain coming into*
*his room, for it was a very rainy night. The Ash leaves lay*
*across the road.*

—

the knock on the door     her lips, my wife
night invisibles the pine

what I trust is true

outside our bedroom window
*very very beautiful the moon*

—

Attention in Ash to Ash
Went into wood to compose
Books composed of leaves
Literal Ash becomes Ash
Book in the fire thrown
Ash attends in Ash to Ash

—

*The Ash leaves lay across the road     The ash in our garden green, one*
*close to it bare the next nearly so     A rainy morning—a whirlwind*
*came that tossed about the leaves & tore off the green leaves of the*

*Ashes*

—

The sparrows below zero
Witness the tree in elegy
Some augury tells me
Survive but do not move

Each blank page a month
Arctic this every January
The sparrows minus zero
In the leafless tree do not

Move they do not move
In me their summer
Nest a vocabulary I do
Not know the words for grass

Dried joined to green pinion
Of mud feather down in inner
Curve tendril twined to twig
Cottonwood seed come out within

Now none nest nowhere
Save within themselves
Wind disheveled no song
The sparrows below zero

Do not move on the branches
Where each sits a music
In notation the whole tree is
Symphony tell me again how

To sing so the ear broods and eye
Coos open a summer coos
Open a summer leaf
A summer leaf in this arctic night

—

confuse my voice with other voices
I write for those others

I know voices river-in and river-to
a heart is a small wind

—

*The lake was still where these breezes were not, but they made it all
alive. I found a strawberry blossom in a rock, the little slender flower
had more courage than the green leaves, for _they_ were but half-expanded
& half grown, but the blossom was spread full out. I uprooted it
rashly, & felt as if I had been committing an outrage, so I planted it
again—it will have a stormy life of it, but let it live if it can.*

3—

*When I seek you out, where do you go?*

—

Irregular, or cobweb—loops in the silk trap prey; no design

Triangular—of which the spider waits outside the web, holding the center string around which the whole web is woven, and when prey enters, pulls the string to collapse the web around it

Funnel—spider waits in the bottom of the web to rush out when prey steps in

Net—spider holds a small web between forelegs and casts it upon the prey it hunts

Orb—spider anchors a first thread to a branch or leaf, and then jumps; where it lands it anchors the first thread. Upon this first silk the whole web will be spun. Many have to be abandoned after one day's use. A certain orb-weaver produces a UV coating on its web that specifically attracts bees, which become entangled, thinking the web is a flower. Some are larger than one foot across. Some are so strong as to be able to entangle birds; others are pulled down by the weight of the morning's dew

—

so bind me to you

I see the sun will
in a single line
bind its whole light

on that spider's thread
silken in the air
finer with its glow

so bind me to you

—

Echo spoke her love in her love's own words. Narcissus spoke to himself
and heard from his lips his own words return. To bend down and kiss
those lips mars the lips—mars the surface with breath. Voice travels
through air by moving the air it travels through. Echo's ear a pond as still
as a mirror that breath moves upon to speak. That lake—inside the ear—
speaks back. Echo's love in love's words. Repetition intones wonder—the
world spoken of in other's words. All spoken and we speak all back.
There are no other words.

I've seen a pond so still it reflects the sky back to itself. I'll speak to you of
it to you. The sky at the bottom of the hill.

—

*Is this thy play,*
*To spin a web out of thyselfe*
*To catch a Fly?*
*For why?*

*I saw a pettish wasp*
*Fall foul therein:*
*Whom yet thy whorle pins did not clasp*
*Lest he should fling*
*His sting.*

*But as afraid, remote*
*Didst stand hereat,*
*And with thy little fingers stroke*
*And gently tap*
*His back.*

—

cloud ripples sky ripples flower leaning out
ripples when the surface is
by the wasp's wings beat

—

The spider in the center sits in the center
Of its mind, the whole orb
Between distant leaves is thoughtless

Geomoetric the dew daily
Collects on strands, the sun in every drop

And when the wasp adheres to thought
Every sun will drop

—

Spin out of myself this web
Anchored to web
Anchored to web the humming
Bird across the world
Is finally a fact
Now its wing is
In my line

—

between a voice and an ear solid air
vibrates a line
molecule, a

word strings itself along sound:

wasp's wings hum a long time
before wasp entangles itself in web

and the web amplifies in struggle the tune

*But he*
*retreats and, fleeing, shouts: "Do not touch me!*
*Don't cling to me! I'd sooner die than say*
*I'm yours!"; and Echo answered him: "I'm yours."*

—

Each one an Echo and Echo myself

*Chaos*　the root in my mouth: silence:
The child's mouth before a tooth breaks through

And then tongue presses against teeth
And speaks a word:

Born into the order of words
(pointing at a tree the mother says, Tree

(pointing still mother says, Branch
(and still, seeing now what the child sees, Nest)

*Nest*　the word echoes
Through centuries my mouth　*This Nest*

Alive with words not spoken by me
Which I repeat back, repeat back

In the world to make my meaning heard

these ancient days so new
I think in my voice    I hear
loved voices speaking to me

—

Gravity and light at equal speed also intertwine, also interact.
The human eye, at the end of telescope, has found regions
in the sky where impossible stars are seen. To gaze up into
night is to gaze backward in time. We nightly see, from where
we are, a "when" in which we did not exist. That light which
denies us is inside us. If we look, there in the far reaches
of space, certain focal points of gravitational forces create
a lens in the vacuum. The lens is made of gravity. To look
through the lens allows us to see further than any eye, with any
telescope, could reach. We look through gravity to see light.

\*

The words fall on the page, a form of gravity the eye reads.
Every word spoken also speaks. Voices speak through it to us,
speak to us of us; these voices that also speak us to ourselves.
A poem forms a lens on a page. We listen to see through it.
We find a world behind the words in which they still live, those
others. Sister and brother in the cottage. The storm blew the
leaves from the ash tree, and some of the leaves still stick to the
windows. We hear ourselves invisible among them, discussing
the pattern of the wet-leaves on glass. To look through a
window is to find one's vision obscured by the world in various
ways. The present tense. A page is a window onto which the
leaves have darkly fallen.

—

ear at the edge of words
alive before I live them

the poem not centered if no

center exists
the already spoken
ancient without choice
and no form if form falsifies
and no pivot if pivot lies

the sparrows build nests each spring
of what material they find

—

*night was come on & the moon was overcast. But as I climbed*
*Moss the moon came out from behind a Mountain Mass of Black*
*Clouds—O the unutterable darkness of the sky & the Earth below*
*the Moon! & the glorious brightness of the moon itself!     The*
*moon retired again & appeared & disappeared several times before*
*I reached home     I had many many exquisite feelings when I saw*
*—it made me more than half a poet.     I was tired when I reached*
*home I could not sit down to reading & tried to write verses but alas!*
*I gave up*

—

Wm composing in the wood
The vision in his sister's eye

*I happened to say that when I was a child*
*I would not have pulled a strawberry blossom*

Caught in the web of Wm's mind
He composed each day in wood

*At dinner-time he came in with the poem*
*Of "Children gathering flowers"*

—

*I took my fence rail spider a handful of flies this morning, but she was out of*
*humor and returned me no thanks. Indeed, she did not feign to notice in any way*
*my contribution to her larder.     I sat down as near the place as practicable,*
*determined to see when the spider would condescend to step out     Finally,*

14

*just as I was about to change my position, to get a closer view, I felt a stinging
sensation    and waving my hand involuntarily before my face, I found myself
cabled, in a flimsy way, to the fence and branches of the tree nearest me    I rose
to go; but not before I had solved the mystery of the motionless spider before me.
Placing my forefinger upon it, to my disgust I found that I had been staring at the
mere ghost of my friend.*

---

*I found that I had been staring*
At one web in which many leaves had landed
In the woods where in my mind I roam

And coming home to dinner found
Myself in the web
Being caught by that I thought to know

---

*The thrush sang almost continually—the little Birds were more than usually busy with their voices.
The sparrows are now full fledged. The nest is so full that they lie upon one another, they sit quietly in
their nest with closed mouths.*

---

the sparrows frantic in the pine
one day song thaws
those wings not shy nor shut
in song each clamors
what is incoherent in ear
the sparrows must hear the world
choral in the pine
the melody each together sings
that at my step beneath the tree
ceases

no song
no
no song

the sun is cold

—

Dorothy in her journal

Echoing Wm     Echoing C     Echoing Anonymous

*We had the Crescent moon with the 'auld moon in her arms'*

# Second

nerve                          *abyss*                          nerve


O—synaptic world—O
love leaps if love too is


—


When praying the Baal Shem Tov trembled and shook. If he prayed
while leaning against a house, the wall his forehead leaned against
trembled and shook with him, as did the wall farthest from him. A
barrel of water touching that farthest wall from the Baal Shem Tov
trembled and shook.

The wood of the barrel side vibrates around the whole circumference of
water. The water vibrates from outer circumference in toward its center.
Where the water ripples it looks thicker. When I speak to you the air behaves
in the same way—rippling thickly into your ear, wave following wave into
meaning, or not. The arms of this galaxy, our spiral galaxy, are formed by
gravitational waves that, like molecules of water gathering within the force
of trembling prayer, bunch stars within the radiating bands of its outspiraling
force. Our own star—yellow sun—burns within the outer extremity of such
an instarred arm. The Milky Way:

That arm shakes and trembles. Every star in it shakes and trembles,
as 150 years ago the Baal Shem Tov leaned his head against a house
and prayed, and now I pray, or hold a sheet of paper in my hands,
a sheet from which I lecture, that in front of my students, with my
voice, shakes and trembles as I hold it. The air shakes. The water
ripples centerward from the shaking barrel's drum.


—

tremor w/
tremor through pine w/
breath nervous w/
breath

—

clamor quiets
blank in wonder
this wonder I am roaming
how I went roaming in my mind

—

*One quantum of light unlinks one molecule, and five rods are needed to perceive the difference. Some stars are at this threshold, and can only be seen by the sides of the eyes.*

—

Orion winters home my eye
To stare too long removes the element
Star the root in both eyes
Periphery where sight quickens into
Constellation
Consideration          both tremble

My pulse sidereal now quick now calm
Like one vast breath punishing pine    love shatters me
I did see the wind in whorl
This winter all winter in my eye
The pine tree trembles in sight a star

Consider the sparrows
Consider the sparrows I love them
Against winter they shiver wings
At night none fly they do not glitter
They tremble in dark air to survive

—

The earth's atmosphere makes the stars glitter. The light through the air is shaken. Some light so old the star that cast it is silent and dead. The eye that sees the light from the dead blue giant looks back at itself from the circumference of the universe. *What you look at looks back at you.* The eye knows, as it sees through the air the star shimmer, not only that it has died, but that soon, in 100 years or 1000, or 1000 more than that, in colors vast and 10 times brighter than any star in the night sky, so bright the star will shine all day in daylight, that the death of the star will supernova into more brilliant sight.

Vision also the shroud of vision.

—

*It is ten years, I think, more or less, since I noticed my sight becoming and growing dim    And even in the morning, if I began as usual to read, I noticed that my eyes felt immediate pain deep within and turned from reading    as often as I looked at a lamp, a sort of rainbow seemed to obscure it. Soon a mist appearing in the left part of the left eye    removed from my sight everything on that side.    The other eye also failing slowly and gradually over a period of almost three years, some months before my sight was completely destroyed, everything which I distinguished when I myself was still seemed to swim, now to the right, now to the left. Certain permanent vapors seem to have settled upon my entire forehead and temples, which press and oppress my eyes with a sort of sleepy heaviness    But I must not omit that, while considerable sight still remained, when I would go to bed and lie on one side or the other, abundant light would dart from my closed eyes; but now, pure black, marked as if with extinguished or ashy light, and as if interwoven with it, pours forth. Yet the mist which always hovers before my eyes both night and day seems always to be approaching white rather than black; and upon the eyes turning, it admits a minute quantity of light as if through a crack.*

—

They tremble darkly in dark air
Wings the earthly element most heavenly
Souls as they shiver expand
A synapse into wider abyss

The pine tree filled with wind
Remains inspired, that limb's
Motion not blown from any lips

Some love beyond order
My eye can't consider and still be mine

Orion is Orion only here
Another angle expands the form past
The mind in winter, no
No home holds

That other orbit where definition blurs
And knowledge stares out
That hypostasis between old stars
*There came new subtlety of eyes*

———

*deep within* I *turned from reading*
the day outside the page
*a sort of rainbow seemed to obscure it*
through which the birds flitted
*with a sort of sleepy heaviness*
their bright bodies *interwoven with it*
some *ashy light* in my eyes
forced me to put down my book
and my ambitions therein
*my eyes both night and day*
and my comfort if comfort it was
I saw in the pages that closing
narrowed the whole day into *a minute*
*quantity of light as if through a crack*
and I had no way to speak of it
and then it was done

———

ash in the eye not ruin

blind the star

*one quantum     the threshold*

others will in deep night shiver

sparrows, stars

*only be seen in the sides of the eyes*

survive through which light

trembles the whole

atmosphere

## 5

*For a long while the spell of the incomprehensible was on the soul.*

—

| | | |
|---|---|---|
| spring the bright veil | * | came down some ash |
| first phoebe bobs in budding | * | of my eyes in my eyes |
| tree   *the command grew* | * | all desolate save the sun |
| *great*   spring the bright | * | a bright disc behind dark |
| veil in falling discloses | * | gauze I wound round my head |
| pearl-in-prism, nectar open | * | some wound I uttered myself |
| O hand the whole horizon's | * | separate from all I see |
| nacre curves   *above the head* | * | "exactly the world, exactly me" |
| *of the man*   habitual in ecstasy | * | some bird's skull leaden rings |
| a phoebe bobs in its budding | * | dull with song the sun a silver |
| song above   *Love all more* | * | coin in empty empyrean afloat |

—

*A globe of gold must barren be,*
*Untill'd and useless: we should neither see*
*Trees, flowers, grass, or corn*
*Such a metallic massy globe adorn:*
*As splendour blinds,*
*So hardness binds;*
*No fruitfulness it can produce;*
*A golden world can't be of any use.*

—

where is our pure
harvest    echo

echo speaks back each
word this clear

syllable opens one half

sound is the thing
that draws things near

the pine tree nears
when sung to it sings

you sing my home
and echo returns

*pine cone:*

a home hangs on a stem
waiting flame

the lodge-pole pine

seeds root in fire
fire calms so tendril sleeps

lightning sings lullaby
cooing softly a name

—

*When he awoke and stepped out of the house, he was free of uncertainty.
All appeared to him simple and definite, and he embraced the world with
his eyes. He said to himself, "Now I know. There are times when the whirl
rushes over the world and shatters its connections, and light and darkness are
no longer separated; then the creatures lose their place and swirl hither and
thither in space. And there are times when heaven holds the earth captive, and
the firmament, which should only separate, transfixes and binds creatures.
But is not all this a reflection and play of time? For now I see that a good
fortune hangs over the things of the world. They live together, undisturbed by
whirl and spell, they walk upright through the wrath of the powers and wait.
Each from its heart performs its part in the world, and has joy in its work.
Creation is indomitable in its felicity."*

*While the rabbi spoke thus to himself, he shut his eyes for happiness. But
when he opened them, the first thing that he saw was the sinking down of an
enormous veil. Then the world lay before him like abyss.*

—

to say you I must embrace
you in your absence
I must love your absence
more than I love you

I can learn to be blank
saying I to abyss
in darkness my delicate "I am"
not in echo

echo predicts the world
will speak back
how find how to say I've seen
what I mean to say

"this world" voids
bliss in
this world

—

I suffered between the seasons. Certain delusions became
wonders. The thaw in the earth I could smell in the air. The
green spears through the loosening loam were in my ear violin
chords, staccato. I saw the music before me. Melody fecund.
Light equals harmony. Morning in song in the trees just now
budding. I saw an *Eastern Phoebe* in a bush. The bird's head
is capped in night, but its breast is morning's palest yellow—
brightest beneath the wings. The first flowers were blue; I did
not know their name. But I wished to speak of them. The first
daffodils...

I sat down to write. The *Phoebe* on the page was and wasn't.
Where is the loosening atmosphere blank as this page is blank?
The bird?—it bobs its tail in the tree because I wound the
spring connected to the key. And when I wrote the flowers
names: each word struck them, and like a gong they rang.

—

| rose in pure element | * | rose in breath blown |
| crush bloom to scent | * | no bliss but in bloom |
| scent to essence crush | * | no bloom save abyss |
| pure element in rose | * | a rose in breath groans |

—

*Another time, in a lowering and sad evening, being alone in the field, when all things were dead and quiet, a certain want and horror fell upon me, beyond imagination. The unprofitableness and silence of the place dissatisfied me, its wideness terrified me, from the utmost ends of the earth fears surrounded me. How did I know but dangers might suddenly arise from the East, and invade me from the unknown regions beyond the seas?*

\*

*Upon this I began to believe   that every thing is indeed as it seemed in my infancy: not as it is commonly apprehended, everything being sublimely rich and great and glorious, every spire of grass   and I in a world where everything is mine, and far better than the greater sort of children esteem diamonds and pearls.*

—

*but dangers might suddenly arise from the East*

*Love has no Why*       o morning       *The definition of melody—is*
arrives in such
thick red
echoes   robes

—

N

W    +    E           *That Definition is none—*

S

6—

This daily everywhere    closed—

*Slowly the ivy on the stones*
*Becomes the stones*

—

A candle alight in the window
doubles flame behind flame
and flame on glass burns equally
cold as night leaning upon the pane
half aglow and I half glow
clothed in black I am the night
singing toward the thought I bear
I am the night of which I sing
but I am not the night
fleeing melody quick as it flees light

—

*who canst thus express*
*A flowery tale more sweetly than our rhyme*

—

*Slowly the ivy*
slowly the flame against
slowly the star against the
slowly the song against the stones
slowly the night against the stones
becomes
slowly the eye against the stones
becomes the
slowly the stones against the stones
becomes the

stones

—

how not remain who is

*unhaunted quite of all but—nothingness?*

—

north no center

looking up and both
are true

out the mouth     out the stone mouth     stone sings stone

sings eye sings night
sings lullaby to stone
stone wakes star

star
sings flame sings sun
sings

ivy from the stone

the all-world ever evergreen

*

Green *Song of* Our Green *Songs*

—

my hand in vineyard is vine, is vineyard
*a garden inclosed is my spouse*
mine are the hind's legs
that leap through arms, her boughs

*a dove in the stairs singing*

and her eyes are doves, coo as doves coo

*peace with work to do*

and dove's wings upon my body blow
flutter at finger's tips
and wheat from the fingertips golden
grows a claret light in the hand

held against the window's light

these leaves open leaves

hands, book, wife-petal, wife-pistil

the tree outside tells us we are the tree's
nestlings:

*Behold, thou art fair, my love; behold, thou art fair;*
*Thou hast dove's eyes.* I have vineyards for hands.

These vineyards are my hands.

—

*But what is greater for us than all enigmatic webs at the margins*
*of being is the central actuality of an everyday hour on earth,*
*with a streak of sunshine on a maple twig and an intimation of*
*the eternal…*

—

Spring the morning I woke

I woke to migration

Dawn the thrush's song

Actual thrush's song in my ear

*Twining of Second Themes*

> *But here there is no light,*
> *Save what from heaven is with the breezes blown*

—

blank in wonder      *      of wonder blank

—

let song double in some other throat

one must grow new before the thunder

he must open new eyes before the thunder
head doubles in height and doubling
a man must sing in two voices
before the warbler returns in wonder
he must open his mother's eyes with his own hand
before his own child points to those drops
of rain so bright with evening
the sun sets beneath the cloud we see
countless suns pour down from thundercloud

—

looking up and both are true

| | | |
|---|---|---|
| less than pip in apple | * | spiderweb white with weed |
| I am in this world | * | blown from pod by breath |
| not seed, not self-seed, | * | by breeze, no tendril, no root |
| not cottonwood, not milkpod | * | in air, not drop by drop to ground |
| not one dandelion seed | * | nor apple bloom minus sound |
| in spiderweb caught | * | minus syllable, minus tongue |
| not weight enough to wake | * | minus eye to read the world's |
| spider's hollow fang I live | * | surface irritation of light |
| beneath hunger I cannot sate | * | cast on what will bear light |
| begging wind again to blow | * | a bitten fruit a fragment in the mind |

*Henceforth, when man is for once overcome by the horror of alienation and the world fills him with anxiety, he looks up (right or left, as the case may be) and sees a picture. Then he sees that the I is contained in the world, and that there is really no I, and thus the world cannot harm the I, and he calms down; or he sees that the world is contained in the I, and that there really is no world, and thus the world cannot harm the I, and he calms down. And when man is overcome again by horror    and the I fills him with anxiety, he looks up and sees a picture; and whichever he sees, it does not matter, either, the empty I is stuffed full of world or it is submerged in the flood of the world, and he calms down.*

*But the moment will come, and it is near, when man, overcome by horror, looks up and in a flash sees both pictures at once. And he is seized by a deeper horror.*

—

A friend of mine studied chaos. She told me the human heart is chaotic. Between the strong beats by which we take our pulse, where the blood courses from vein into ventricle and ventricle into arch, the electric current by which the heart-muscle contracts can still be measured. An EKG graphically shows us this current: the peaks and valleys of that line in you—it looks almost like a thrush's song. An unhealthy heart, in between beats, maintains a constant current. The more regular the electric pulse the closer the heart is to arrest.

*The heart, nurtured in the seas of rebounding blood, / where most especially is what is called thought by humans, / for the blood round the heart in humans is thought.*

The healthy heart, between pulses, between pulses that maintain the pressure by which blood fills the body—the healthy heart is chaotic between every beat. The pattern cannot be predicted. Thinking chaotic between two points. Blood as song. The healthy heart lives in chaos.

—

*what has been spoken has not*
*been said:*

we speak of the world
in words that are not the world
and then the world is "ours"

—

hours blow heaven below these clouds
a raindrop ripples force in circles to shore
but also shakes the depths—my throat
in sediment, soft sift, my throat in silt—

some spiders weave below the dock
near the shore, some in the bushes away—

wind through the orb-weaver's web will it
remember my throat vibrating with words
I shook to tell you?      *Love has no Why*

Void void by embracing void—the spilt arm
nightly the milky way proves all is
already done

here is a *star*, Kristy, in darkest ink—
it is a star none before now have seen—
somewhere it trembles in light
not as now, dark to be seen against a page's white

breath in speaking it might blow it out
how you learn to see it is its name
you have a nerve, and nerves will flame
at touch, touch the page, speak it—

(it's there in the pine outside the window)

*O, sparrow*     [speak the bird's o until all breath runs out]

—

sparrow swift spring
do blossoms seed
my voice among voices
world-spoken self
and then I am speaking

voices inside my voice
sparrow spring is swift
blossoms seed and clothe
the world floats in abyss
but world still will be
many voices on my lip

—

Some birds snatch cobwebs from corners to help hold together their nests.
Stitch dead grass to new dead grass. Stitch sere to green. Nestling hatched
in silk on which the imago died. The human heart among a nest of veins.
The nestling learns a two note song of infinite variation. We learn to sing
what the blood thinks.

—

systole
———
diastole                    (pulse, pulse, pulse)        *< DIAPASON >*

# Third

the command grows loud
my heart anxious with a heart
spell the incomprehensible
grackle and nothing perched
in the pine every word
pulses with error but error is true
the grackle with the infant heart's
chaos in his mouth
patience akin to wonder
the heart astray in the pine
patience finds a way in
patience astray in the pine

—

Falling into the earth but by the earth embraced
The world ensnares, even bare, even divorced
Of green, of ivy bright, of midnight in the oak,
Of light beneath the wave in waves
As the lake shallows to nothing, as the lake
Shallows to a stone it swallowed, and the stone
Swallows itself in dust, and I am this dust,
And my wife this dust latched to dust
We love. The earth falling at equal speed
Into the sun. The sun falling into nothing
At the galaxy's core. The compass point
On which the needle spins is soldered
To abyss. The jailer's keys float beyond
Us on an orbit's ring. None beg mercy
But mercy comes. Mercy bounds, it binds.
This grave falling drones beneath our song.
The lock turned echoes through the prison's hall
Forever, gear turning, single metal note's no-song
Ringing…Do you hear it? That droning note
Whose sound is nothing? Against it we speak
Such words, against nothing our melody is heard.

*Wistful and wondering, she would sit in summer weather by the high fender in the Lodge, looking up at the sky through the barred window, until bars of light would arise, when she turned her eyes away, between her and her friend, and she would see him through a grating, too.*

*"Thinking of the fields," the turnkey said once, after watching her, "ain't you?"*

*"Where are they?" she enquired.*

*"Why they're—over there, my dear," said the turnkey, with a vague flourish of his key. "Just about there."*

*"Does anybody open them, and shut them? Are they locked?"*

—

these bars of green wheat
will be golden in a month

the bars will brittle
our mouths full with nothing

nothing
questions us the questioners

under oath the oats claim bliss
the husk abyss

to lengthen the verdict
we plead innocence

*Two prisoners whose cells adjoin communicate with each other by knocking on the wall. The wall is the thing which separates them but it is also their means of communication. Every separation is a link.*

—

a key turning in the fields    turns
a key wild in the wild rose    a child
in the rose    *every thought is...*    morning
red through the prison bars all noon
a grave gathers in the opening dew

these gallows are rose in hue    this lock
doubles a child    born in debt    in prison
as I myself was born    *every heaven is also . . .*
through the window's bars the field
and the field-sparrow is a prison in flight

two white bars on each wing    my mind
is a little key in a child's hand    turning
the rose to tune the rose    West
a single petal at day's end is the whole
sky this dying    bloom the barred    clouds

bruised white    when the moon rises    the moon
is not light but seems made of light
the moon is a prison floating in the night
a key is bloody in shadow but also bright
in orbit turning    pointing vaguely    on the field    it shines

—

*...also a prison;*

holding hands w/
in love w/

*...a prison*

—

I find myself, when I leave my basement office in the
museum at which I work, wandering longer through
galleries few visit. I stare at objects in glass cases—
removed from time for being touched so long by time.
Chinese *Tomb-Figurines*. A pair of ceramic dancing
women whose wooden hands, keeping delicate time to
the music none hear, are decayed and gone. A juggler
balances an absent globe on his nose; now he laughing
stares up into the stars, his mouth agape, and where
the globe attached by a wooden peg, a hole deep in his
forehead. His belly is filled with ash or nothing. Coil
pots I've held—built and fired 3000 years ago. I've put
my hand into the mouth and felt the coil wall smoothed
by the potter's hand, put my fingers in the fingerprints
left by him now gone, pressing against the wall to make
it sound. *Every separation is a link.* The celadon vase a
small green lake in my eye; but nearing, the curves are
cracked, the glaze a broken network, as of veins, across
the surface. My eye draws lines along those lines. And
last, the pillows—each ceramic—called *Bean-Shaped
Pillow, Tiger-Shaped Pillow, Cloud-Shaped Pillow...*

> I think in bed, staring up into the whole night balanced on my
> head, my mouth open, my mouth agape

> > I've laid my head down
> > on Tiger
> > and I've laid my head
> > on Cloud

> and both were hard as stone
> and both were Tiger and Cloud

39

mortal June minds June wild

wild June yields June mild

mild June prays June fevered

fevered June begs June's trial

to humble my eye I double my
eye    note the water strider's orb
this sphere sings that I must sing
each leg on tense water stands
on each leg to draw its circle just
a single stone is saintly study
circular & small    note in hand
it skips across the same river
it sinks in when thrown
the firefly above the river at night
glows bright twice    note I see
stars on still water dim when struck
substellar light beacons as precise
in air above mirrored in water below
I double vision to see this world
this world more seen is less known

—

*A stone presses downward and manifests its heaviness. But while
this heaviness exerts an opposing pressure upon us it denies us any
penetration into it. If we attempt such a penetration by breaking open
the rock, it still does not display in its fragments anything inward that
has been opened up.    Color shines and wants only to shine.    When
we analyze it in rational terms    it is gone. It shows itself only when
it remains undisclosed and unexplained.*

Resolves to write nothing
but "what I see"

I see noon on the blank page
noon whitens the water the water beetle's
script in wakes
the page by its own current will erase

draw nearer to read but cannot read
the sentence sounds
like doom soft in the reeds
while the lilypad blooms

two darning needles smooth in blue
shadow with wings
each precisely aligned with each
this mirror hovers in the air

Resolved to write nothing
but "what I know"

—

The reed exactly doubles
Humility speaking twice in water
Once by wind and once by mirror
Adds itself to itself
To make its true length known

—

*It required some rudeness to disturb with our boat the mirror-like surface of the water, in which every twig and blade of grass was so faithfully reflected; too faithfully indeed for art to imitate, for only Nature may exaggerate herself. The shallowest still water is unfathomable. Wherever the trees and skies are reflected, there is more than Atlantic depth, and no danger of fancy running aground. We noticed that it required a separate intention of the eye, a more free and abstracted vision, to see the river bottom merely; and so there are manifold visions in the direction of every object, and even the most opaque reflect the heavens from their surface.*

—

Bend down my head to look up.
Bend closed my hands to make a cup.
Bend myself to the river.
In shallows there the cranes are flying.
Those ripples are not their wings.
Those ripples are my hands put through the birds

To drink. Be quiet, be still. Those are the cranes
Flying across the sky cupped in my hands.
Those ripples are not their pulsing wings.

Those ripples blurring the birds are the bird's
Wings in my wrist, in my breast, that river
In which the ruddy duck rests, the tanager rests,

And the house-finch's red song
Sings from the ventricle it roosts in for nest.
There are the cranes flying in my hands

Before I drink. And then I drink. And then
The mourning dove coos. And then the cranes
Solve the parch. Their throats cool

My throat. I cannot sing their song for you.
Here it was, in my hands—these hands are yours
—empty as the air those wings strove through.

—

               resolved nothing but not
               pray how not to
               darken shadow with thought
               resolved to nothing but
               what upon us denies us
               entrance pray open the
               river first open the rock

—

Nine months now nesting in these pages. Blank days mirror me.
I went to the river to escape. I saw the darning needles flying.
They mate in the air. The male clasping the female by her neck
with a pincer on his tail. I heard their wings beat against each
other beating against the pine tree to fly up over the water. They
were a circle in the air. I bent my head to the water. I could see
on the surface, above the riverweed flagging forward with the
current, my own face in echo. *When I seek you out, where do you go?*
So easy to betray what it is I think I see. Name the stone and
like a white flower on the riverbank the stone will wither. Name

the crane and the crane will sink like stone. But some other grace bridges both worlds—I can see it when I look backward at myself, bent to the river those weeks ago, even now, with my pen on this page. My head bent down to my own head on the water, and in the dark space, the negative space between my profile and my profile's reflection, there is the chalice if one can see it, air soldered to water, into which the whole world pours its prayer, pours its presence, and once full, out the mouth runneth over.

—

shadow motion all

*the unbribable charity*

who puts his wrist in water

so water takes his pulse

the darning needles fly

in perfect attention to

the other's wings I'll illustrate

all old wives tell this tale

the darning needles sew up the ears

of truant schoolboys

so they could not hear the bells

can you hear the bells

ringing behind a door

9—

*first*

sparrow  rose   pine   ash
sparrow  rose   pine   ash

green    abyss  ivy    wasp
green    abyss  ivy    wasp

thrush   wake   spider star
thrush   wake   spider star

*

*& then*

sparrow  rose   pine   ash
green    abyss  ivy    wasp
thrush   wake   spider star

—

*my facts shall be falsehoods*

my sparrows shall brood
in rose my pine shall be
a stem (as hers) a thorn shall hold
in thrall the sky my ivy twined
around my wrists my pulse
an arbor over me my spider
shall walk upon the echo caught

Imagine thus the pond: a bell
filled with water. Atmosphere first
walked upon by water-striders.
Where their legs touch the water
a cloud is dimpled. Paperwhites
lean into vision. Echo is a figure round;
*her wilderness is a greenwood.*
Echo enlarged is ecstasy. The music
in the leaves is first found below
the mirror on the pond. A leaf is
slow in the air as it falls. Then heaven
trembles. This is not terror—words.
Then the paperwhites cannot see.
To dip a pen in cloud undoes the cloud.
Strike the bell and the sky parts.
Or love-cracked, bending
over the still water, peering through
my own gaze peering back at me,
I see how erasure ecstatic undoes
the surface by which the world was seen.
Bells in circles ring and so their sound.
Imagine thus the pond:
There is a tongue under the water.

—

a bell-tone blown vibrant on breeze
my wasp shall be honey's viceroy
in me her wilderness shall deny
as greenwood does flame
my star shall be bright to shatter
my song in tendrils grows
woods deep in dictionary where the aster
springs rootless upward into bliss
my music shall bewilder my own
heart shall be falsehood

*to common sense*

—

*I saw a snake by the roadside and touched him with my foot to see if he were alive. He had a toad in his jaws, which he was preparing to swallow with his jaws distended to three times his width, but he relinquished his prey in haste and fled; and I thought, as the toad jumped leisurely away with his slime-covered hind-quarters glistening in the sun, as if I, his deliverer, wished to interrupt his meditations—without a shriek or fainting—I thought what a healthy indifference he manifested. Is not the broad earth still? he said.*

—

what I have been doing is trying to listen
by opening my mouth
*
this year in these pages
*
found the slough of the snake on the road-side
and only then the snake

—

*Echo*, I pine.                    *        *o* pine

Looking up. Over the water. My voice    *    watermyvoice
has no edge. I am the edge. I pin       *    I am    edging
My voice to a leaf. The water is        *    leafthaw   eros

45

| | | |
|---|---|---|
| not thin. Light betrays the surface. | * | inlight yourface |
| Will you be seen? Over the water. | * | bein      water |
| A wave is thin. The shore is no sound. | * | away   is   now |
| Pine bough the empty sleeve. I am | * | empty      eve |
| Looking up. My voice. If I am alone. | * | voice  my   own |

| | | |
|---|---|---|
| I pine, *Return.* | * | in *Return* |

—

The night star-filled; the day filled with a star. Deeper in the page the word multiplies. Star: to crack, to break. The day filled with a fracture; the night…The night, when most I mean to lift my words back into the thought they fell from, is dark ink dried in a glass bowl. Constellations give us their awful clue. Night's but an ink-pot buoyed in a greater blank—some author writes nothing deeper on nothing, at the nib's tip, some light breaks through.

—

*The eye is the first circle; the horizon which it forms is the second      Our life is an apprenticeship to the truth that around every circle another can be drawn      there is always another dawn risen on mid-noon      under every deep a lower deep opens*

—

clamor at ecstasy but ecstasy
sings the blank
space on the page between each
word is Lethe
exquisite when spoken true

First I learned to forget how the clouds billowing into storm took other shapes—the thunderhead as the sparrow's wing, the tulip wilting, the toad with bulbous eyes—and see only the cloud itself. Noted in my journal how the wind in upper atmosphere can bend a wisp into a circle. Noted the spring congests into storms, the clouds progressing by circular upwellings, as of a liquid boiling, and the underedge of each node a darker gray limned in blue, the shadow by which the cloud grows in definition.

> exquisite when spoken each word
> rings with one note
> Orion plucks on his shimmering
> bow vibrates also in the bough
> of the pine and the worm
> which feasts on the pine as it grows

Then forgot the words to the clear tone. Then forgot to speak. Then my blood vibrated with the working of the tree. Then a book was leaves on water, spread out, so the water couldn't be seen. Then ecstasy rippled. Then the stars were on the water. Then I looked up. Then I forgot the constellations—Orion, Hydra, Dipper, Bear—and only saw the light piercing through the dark. Then I had no story but this poem.

—

*All I can say is that I live and
breathe and have my thoughts.*

—

> we are this still
> earth a dark toad in the mouth
> of a snake and the snake's mouth
> upon us is light

dawn clangs shut another day
keyhole rising to noon
our sentence is to be without shadow
a minute each day light shackles
claims the judge
you'll see and you will be seen

\*

*the wild and the tame are one*

\*

my thoughts pacing behind bars

—

| | | a mortal blossom and a blossom untold | | |

| | | pointing vaguely at the fields with a key | | |

| | | here are the fetters, the lock & spring | | |

never asked but granted release
so I asked myself to roam
cuffed in song, bars in my eyes
from being behind bars so long
a convict walking to find a wall

the pine tree solid but I could see
lines along which it could fold
and folding be a paper pine to delight
a child rooted in a child's hand

but nearing the hidden sparrows sang
the crow echoed unseen
and walking beneath the tree I found
the warden cooing
the pine dropped down its scent

on me the whole wonder entraps
so I ceased and my mind ceased

and my mind's method, self-cruel,
self-vaunting, and begged my sentence
longer: bewilderment & patience

—

*I hear faintly the cawing of a crow far, far away, echoing from unseen
wood-side    It mingles with the slight murmur of the village, the sound
of children at play, as one stream empties gently into another, and the
wild and the tame are one    It is not merely crow calling to crow, for
it speaks to me too. I am part of one great creature with him; if he has
voice, I have ears    On the one hand, it may be, is the sound of children
at school saying their a, b, ab's, on the other, far in the wood-fringed
horizon, the cawing of the crows    out at their long recess, children who
have got dismissed*

—

    a)   bee in the snapdragon

    b)   train distant on the tracks

    c)   train inside the blossom hums

    &

    d)   bee transports pollen's freight

—

*Unless the humming of a gnat is as the music of the
spheres, and the music of the spheres as the humming
of a gnat, they are naught to me.*

—

Narcissus, the flower, also called the *Paperwhite*. And myself,
holding the petals. The blank page reflects. The pond could not
hold Echo's voice, but ink does. Every word mine equally yours.
Nothing here has not been spoken before. But peering through the
deepening pages, I think I see my own reflection.

Patience lets the dark mud settle. Each word says: You are seeking me. Narcissus could not speak—breath would blow his image away in ripples.

Echo is only breath. Words threaten what we see. What we love to see we think we love to see.

There on the pond, the sparrows in the pine unseen, the pine unseen, the surface filled with sky, my head the forefront of heaven, and the paperwhites leaning in behind me, until breath echoes louder, *seek me out where I go*, and the wind through the petals is the rustling of pages written on stems, and when louder echo blows, volumes break and suddenly blank, with the breeze make away.

And one decides, I decide, whether or not to look up, whether to stand, whether to seek (myself who once was sought), to find Echo clothed in pages, to kiss Echo in her vellum robes.

—

night not the night / echoes / these words
not words / turnkey / echoes / dark ink

on page / this legible / prison a book
isn't night / but night's color / this ink

shackles sense to sense / listen to
my hand / this prisonyard / full of song

the pond enchained / heaven / in echo
but heaven broke / free

not this / not this word / these words / no book
can / as nothing from nothing / flee

I have no defense / but one plea
*a wild innocence not ease* / must sing

the sparrow / a convict / in my throat
no torn page will / release

to tear the page / is perjury
and perjured song / will cease

*every separation / echo / is a link*
every book a prison / turnkey

every prison / a nest

—

*Lying on his back, he gazed up now into the high, cloudless sky. "Do I not know that that is infinite space, and that it is not a rounded vault? But, however I screw up my eyes and strain my sight, I cannot see it but as round and finite, and in spite of my knowing about infinite space, I am incontestably right when I see a firm blue vault, far more right than when I strain my eyes to see beyond it."*

*ceased thinking, and only, as it were, listened to mysterious voices that seemed talking joyfully and earnestly within him.*

*"Can this be faith?" he thought, afraid to believe     and with both hands brushing away the tears that filled his eyes.*

—

ceased thinking / *my sweete delight* / and only listened

*

sparrow's / tremblestar / song

*

Lett me but kisse thyne eyes     My sparrow

*

cannot faith be broken and still be

*

harm be harmony

51

> *There is a dark*
> *Invisible workmanship that reconciles*
> *Discordant elements, and*

no cosmos
in a child's mouth before a tooth
stars through the gum and consonant
the tongue lives on lack
first chaos ripens silent in the mouth
vacuum considers star // a first word
speaks of what he does not have
as light must cross abyss so a word
on breath crosses through a child's lips
once and then the world appears
receding in echo an order more vast
the distant flees at greatest speed
her voice in red-shift the infant cries
come back // the white light is dim
"I am here" I want to say "It is mine"
some blue light throbbing in my throat
the mouth orders the heart be silent
a pulse is patience
consider the wrist the ankle the throat
the finger's tip a constellation
twinned with wife we are a web
I feel my pulse with my eye
the eye draws lines webbing all
to all // saccadic motion // the eye
in echo the page read but not words
the thin grass webbed to thin grass
nests the page
and reading Thoreau on the train
into the city // going to work // to teach
I look up from "sparrow" to see sparrow
sparrows in the cemetery // the lightning
struck tree // the broken wood still fresh
the leaves will all be torn see my hands
pulsing this is not the wind

blowing // there is no wind // an eye
weaves by leaping into nothing // a word
by silken tie tethers world to world
and one note sung at highest pitch is enough
to thrill the vibrating whole into song
this is no single voice // there is the grocery list
from winter sewn into the sparrow's nest
here are the pages in which I nest
*Those sparrows, too, are thoughts I have.*
*They come and go; they flit by quickly*
*On their migrations…I know not whither*
*Or why exactly. One will not rest*
*Upon its twig for me …The whole*
*Copse will be alive with my rambling thoughts,*
*Bewildering me…*that tree // my mind
nests // in the starlings // of the raucous
chest stippled white against black feathers
the bird's breast mimics the night sky
the starling mimics other bird's songs
not quite perfectly // here I am // I am alive
today // all I mean to say // I say
when I neared the tree the whole tree flew
hundreds of black birds against the sky
occupying but a few feet in the air
flying in a single motion a single mind
the dark surface fluctuating in size
was this the widow's shroud my vision
feared // tumbling through the air // not
blown by wind but by song blown
until suddenly each bird unwove itself
and the mourning cloth dispersed:
There is the sky // It is blue //
Beneath it the good green earth lives //
I had no other thought. Here I dwell.

Notes


1—


Dorothy Wordsworth, *The Grasmere Journal*
Shakespeare, *Cymbeline*


2—


Dorothy Wordsworth, *The Grasmere Journal*


3—


Ovid, *Metamorphoses*
Edward Taylor, "Upon a Spider Catching a Fly"

*Twining of First Themes*

Dorothy Wordsworth, *The Grasmere Journal*
Charles C. Abbott, *An October Diary*


4—


Ronald Johnson, *ARK*
John Milton, *Letter: To Leonard Philarus, Athenian; Westminster, Sept. 28, 1654*
Ezra Pound, "Canto LXXXI"


5—


Martin Buber, *The Legend of the Ba'al Shem*
Thomas Traherne, "A Globe of Gold Must Barren Be"
Martin Buber, *The Legend of the Ba'al Shem*
Thomas Traherne, *Centuries of Meditation*
Meister Eckhart, *Sermons*
Emily Dickinson, "849"

6—

Wallace Stevens, "The Man with the Blue Guitar"
John Keats, "Ode on a Grecian Urn"
John Keats, "Ode on Indolence"
Song of Songs
Martin Buber, *I & Thou*

*Twining of Second Themes*

John Keats, "Ode to a Nightingale"
Martin Buber, *I & Thou*
Empedocles

7—

Charles Dickens, *Little Dorritt*
Simone Weil, *Metaxu*
Ralph Waldo Emerson, "The Poet"

8—

Martin Heidegger, "The Origin of the Work of Art"
Henry David Thoreau, *A Week on the Concord and Merrimack Rivers*
Henry David Thoreau, *Selections from Thoreau's Journals*

9—

Henry David Thoreau, *Selections from Thoreau's Journals*
Ralph Waldo Emerson, "Circles"

*Twining of Third Themes*

Henry David Thoreau, *Selections from Thoreau's Journals*
Leo Tolstoy, *Anna Karenina*
William Shakespeare, *The Life of Timon of Athens*

*Twining of Twinings*

William Wordsworth, *The Prelude*
Henry David Thoreau, *Selections from Thoreau's Journals*